Fred and Jen Jumped

A Division of The McGraw·Hill Companies

Columbus, Ohio

www.sra4kids.com

SRA/McGraw-Hill

A Division of The **McGraw·Hill** *Companies*

Send all inquiries to:
SRA/McGraw-Hill
8787 Orion Place
Columbus, OH 43240-4027

ISBN 0-07-569831-5
    3 4 5 6 7 8 9 DBH 05 04 03 02

Fred led Jen in a new sport.
Fred jumped.
Jen jumped.

Fred dipped.
Jen dipped.

Fred jogged.
Jen jogged.

Fred stepped.
Jen stepped.

Fred hopped.
Jen hopped.

Jen flipped.
Fred rested.